Caseload and Workload Management

U.S. Department of Health and Human Services,
Administration for Children and Families, Anonymous

Child Welfare Information Gateway
PROTECTING CHILDREN ■ STRENGTHENING FAMILIES

ISSUE BRIEF

April 2010

Caseload and Workload Management

Large caseloads and excessive workloads in many jurisdictions make it difficult for child welfare workers to serve families effectively. The average caseload for child welfare workers often exceeds recommended levels, sometimes by double or more (Alliance for Children and Families, American Public Human Services Association [APHSA], & Child Welfare League of America [CWLA], 2001). The complexity of cases requiring intensive intervention, as well as administrative requirements, further adds to a caseworker's workload. Manageable caseloads and workloads can make a real difference in a worker's ability to spend adequate time with children and families, improve staff retention, and ultimately have a positive impact on outcomes for children and families.

What's Inside:

- Definitions
- Benefits of Caseload and Workload Management
- Catalysts and Motivating Factors
- Workload Studies and Other Tools
- Strategies for Caseload and Workload Management
- State and Local Examples of Caseload and Workload Strategies
- Related Resources
- References

U.S. Department of Health and Human Services
Administration for Children and Families
Administration on Children, Youth and Families
Children's Bureau

Child Welfare Information Gateway
Children's Bureau/ACYF
1250 Maryland Avenue, SW
Eighth Floor
Washington, DC 20024
800.394.3366
Email: info@childwelfare.gov
www.childwelfare.gov

Reducing and managing caseloads and workloads are not simple tasks for child welfare administrators. Agencies face a number of challenges, including negotiating budget crises and hiring freezes, addressing worker turnover, finding qualified applicants for open positions, implementing time-intensive best practices, and managing multiple reforms simultaneously (Day & Peterson, 2008). Even the basic determination of what caseloads and workloads currently are and what they should be can be thorny.

Nevertheless, States are addressing these challenges and successfully implementing a variety of strategies to make caseloads and workloads more manageable. Approaches range from adding and retaining staff to improving worker effectiveness to implementing system improvements.

In an effort to build the workload knowledge base and share lessons learned across States, this information brief provides State child welfare managers with an overview of:

- The benefits of caseload and workload management

- Catalysts and motivating factors

- Workload studies and other tools

- Strategies for caseload and workload management

- State and local examples of caseload and workload strategies

- Related resources

DEFINITIONS

- **Caseload:** The number of cases (children or families) assigned to an individual worker in a given time period. Caseload reflects a ratio of cases (or clients) to staff members and may be measured for an individual worker, all workers assigned to a specific type of case, or all workers in a specified area (e.g., agency or region).

- **Workload:** The amount of work required to successfully manage assigned cases and bring them to resolution. Workload reflects the average time it takes a worker to (1) do the work required for each assigned case; and (2) complete other non-casework responsibilities.

Benefits of Caseload and Workload Management

Caseload and workload management often appear as key ingredients in a State's comprehensive strategy to produce better outcomes for children and families. The benefits of reasonable caseloads and manageable workloads relate to:

- **Retaining staff and reducing turnover.** Heavy caseloads and workloads have been cited repeatedly as key reasons that workers leave the child welfare workforce (Zlotnik, DePanfilis, Daining, & Lane, 2005; U.S. General Accounting Office [GAO],

2003; Gonzalez, Faller, Ortega, & Tropman, 2009; Ellett, A. J., Ellet, C. D., & Rugutt, 2003; Social Work Education Consortium, 2002).

- **Delivering quality services.** High staff turnover resulting from heavy caseloads can have a negative impact on the timeliness, continuity, and quality of services provided by an agency (National Council on Crime and Delinquency, 2006; Strolin, McCarthy, & Caringi, 2007; Flower, McDonald, & Sumski, 2005; GAO, 2003).

- **Engaging families and building relationships.** Essential child welfare processes—including family engagement, relationship building, assessment, and permanency planning—are time intensive and require frequent worker-client contact. Heavy workloads and caseloads reduce the amount of time available for these processes.

- **Positive outcomes for children and families.** Workloads and caseloads have been linked to performance on Federal Child and Family Services Reviews (CFSRs) and achievement of safety and permanency outcomes (Children's Bureau, 2006; GAO, 2003).

Catalysts and Motivating Factors

Some States set out specifically to reduce caseloads and workloads; others have reforms imposed on them; and still others arrive at caseload and workload reduction as an unintended effect of other initiatives. The impetus for caseload and workload

reduction efforts typically emerges from one or more of the following catalysts:

- **CFSRs.** After the first round of CFSRs, about half the States' Program Improvement Plans (PIPs) noted the need for improvements in workloads or caseloads (Children's Defense Fund and Children's Rights, 2006). States continue to address workloads/caseloads and related issues (e.g., recruitment, retention, training, supervision, and systems reform) in the second round PIPs as a means to improve CFSR outcomes and to achieve compliance with Federal standards.

- **Legislation.** Several State legislatures have mandated State and local jurisdictions to assess workload issues, meet identified standards, implement specific strategies such as hiring additional staff, and report on progress. For examples of existing legislation, see Delaware, Florida, Indiana, and Texas .

- **Litigation and consent decrees.** Class-action litigation across the country—frequently resulting from high-profile fatalities—has brought attention to child welfare system reform and generated workforce improvements (Farber & Munson, 2007). Provisions in settlement agreements and consent decrees often require jurisdictions (for example, Baltimore, MD; District of Columbia; Illinois; and Milwaukee, WI) to meet specific caseload standards.

- **Staffing needs.** In a nationwide survey, State administrators identified reducing caseloads, workloads, and supervisory ratios as the most important action for child welfare agencies to take to retain qualified frontline staff (APHSA, 2005).

- **Standards and accreditation.** When developing caseload management strategies, some States and localities take into consideration the caseload standards and guidance recommended by CWLA; others strive to meet the Council on Accreditation (COA) standards in order to achieve accreditation. States have had varying success in achieving and maintaining these standards.

- **Systems reform.** Currently, some States are engaged in developing new practice models and implementing systemwide reform efforts, such as differential response, family engagement, and system of care initiatives. While caseload/workload reduction may not be a stated goal of these reform efforts, it sometimes is a necessary component or a resultant outcome.

- **Union negotiations.** Unions representing child welfare workers have played an important role in negotiating improved caseload ratios.

Workload Studies and Other Tools

The process of caseload and workload management often begins with workload and time studies. These studies analyze how work is being done and how time is spent, and frequently compare the actual data with estimations of what is needed to deliver quality services and best practices. Workload studies can provide a foundation for:

- Determining how many workers are needed to handle cases effectively in different program areas and then setting caseload standards and staff allocations accordingly

- Understanding how much time workers spend on providing services to clients, documenting their work, completing other administrative tasks, traveling, etc., and then identifying more efficient processes and practices

- Exploring how various case characteristics (such as risk levels, number of siblings, immigrant status) can influence workload and assessing workflow implications (Tooman & Fluke, 2002)

- Managing work expectations, which can lead to higher work satisfaction and boost staff morale (Edwards & Reynolds, 2008)

- Justifying resource allocations and building stakeholder support for caseload/workload management strategies

Often working with expert consultants, many States and counties across the country have conducted workload studies using various methodologies to address their workforce issues. Several States are now moving from point-in-time studies to periodic and automated tracking of workloads and caseloads to inform ongoing workforce decisions. Analytic tools, like those used in Minnesota and New Jersey, serve as further supports to routinely assess caseload data and their implications for staffing and workflow management.

In other States and counties, however, it has not been feasible for cost, time, or other reasons to conduct workload studies. These jurisdictions can still improve their workforce management by learning from other workload study findings to approximate their staffing

This material may be freely reproduced and distributed. However, when doing so, please credit Child Welfare Information Gateway. Available online at www.childwelfare.gov/pubs/case_work_management/

4

and workforce needs (Wagner, Johnson, & Healy, 2008).

Strategies for Caseload and Workload Management

Strategies to reduce caseloads and workloads include targeted efforts as well as broader initiatives in three categories: staffing, improving worker effectiveness, and implementing program and practice changes.

Staffing

Manageable caseloads and workloads are functions in large part of the number of qualified staff available to handle cases. Caseload/workload strategies related to staffing reflect:

- **Recruitment of new staff.** Agencies are implementing a range of activities to attract qualified applicants, including adopting new outreach strategies, revising hiring practices, offering higher salaries, and providing stipends for bilingual staff or for masters in social work. While adding staff may be the most obvious approach to reducing caseloads and workloads, it often is constrained by available funding and the lack of qualified applicants for open positions. Several States that have added large numbers of new positions (e.g., Delaware, Indiana, and New Jersey) have been supported by legislation or consent decrees.

- **Retention of existing staff.** To reduce turnover—which is both a consequence and a cause of high workloads—agencies are introducing employee recognition and reward programs, providing mentoring initiatives, enhancing supervision and support, enabling job sharing and flex time, and offering opportunities for professional development and advanced education. In addition, retention efforts include practices intended to improve the match between the worker and the job through competency-based hiring (Bernotavicz, 2008), internships, and use of videos that provide recruits with a more realistic view of child welfare work (for examples, see Realistic Job Preview Videos from Colorado, Maine, and North Carolina. Many States also are conducting exit interviews to determine why staff leave and using findings to inform new retention initiatives (Robison, 2006).

- **Reallocation of staff.** In some instances, agencies (e.g., in Maryland and Idaho) have been reallocating staff to more efficiently address workloads and caseload distribution. In making reallocation and case assignment decisions, States may consider not only the number of cases but also the type of case and level of effort required.

- **Specialized and support staff.** Some States develop specialized staff units or positions to allocate workloads more efficiently; others assign support staff to help lessen caseworker paperwork and administrative tasks.

For more research-based and practical "how-to" information on recruitment and retention strategies used in the field, see:

- *Strategies Matrix Approach to Recruitment and Retention Techniques (SMARRT Manual), produced by the Western Regional Recruitment and Retention Project*

- *Training Series: Staff Retention in Child and Family Services developed by Michigan State University School of Social Work*

- *Workforce Tools featured on the Child Welfare Information Gateway website*

Improving Worker Effectiveness

Agencies also address workload management through practices that aim to improve the efficiency and effectiveness of workers, so that once in place, staff can handle more cases or work in less time. Strategies include:

- **Training and professional development.** Well-trained staff are able to complete tasks accurately and in a timely manner. In addition, studies suggest that educational programs provide workers with both competencies and increased commitment to their jobs, which are associated with retention (Zlotnik et al., 2005). Agencies are delivering a variety of training initiatives to build competencies and align skills with new practice models. Some States have formed university-agency partnerships that provide training and, in some cases, funding for child welfare staff to pursue graduate social work degrees (e.g., New York's Social Work Education Consortium).

- **Supervision.** Good supervision helps workers gain knowledge and build the skills needed to conduct their work more effectively and efficiently. In addition, research points to supportive supervision as a critical factor in reducing turnover (Zlotnik et al., 2005; Juby & Scannapieco, 2007; GAO, 2003.) Agencies are working to reduce staff/supervisor ratios, build supervisor skills, and improve the supervisor-caseworker relationship through supervisory training, coaching initiatives, mentoring opportunities, and feedback mechanisms.

- **Design teams.** Bringing together staff of every level from frontline workers and supervisors up through managers and administrators, design teams in New York State and elsewhere are used first to identify workforce issues and their causes and then to develop and implement workable solutions.

- **Tools and technology.** Agencies are using current technologies and mobile devices to help workers document casework more efficiently, access information that supports decision-making, and make use of waiting time. For example, workers in parts of Texas, Wisconsin, and Oklahoma take tablet PCs into the field to aid in streamlined documentation; workers in Vermont carry cell phones that not only offer telephone service but also email, scheduling, and modem functions; and workers in Iowa are using SACWIS as a case management tool and resource for decision-making.

- **Quality assurance.** States and localities are implementing case review processes and quality assurance efforts to ensure effectiveness.

Implementing Program and Practice Changes

While some States focus on enlarging or enhancing the workforce, others approach caseload/workload management by reducing the "work," i.e., decreasing the number of children and families who enter, reenter, or remain in the system.

- **Prevention and early intervention.** Agencies seek to reduce the number of cases entering the child welfare system through in-home and other prevention services as well as differential/alternative response initiatives. Arizona and Idaho are among the States that recognize prevention and early intervention as part of their workload/caseload management strategies.

- **Permanency initiatives.** Other States and jurisdictions—for example, Suffolk County, New York (Levy Credits Foster Care, 2009)—focus on the backend of the system, employing initiatives related to kinship care, adoption, and other avenues to permanency as a means to reduce caseloads.

- **Other systems reforms.** While systemwide reforms such as new practice models and systems of care may not always be identified as caseload/workload management, they can, nevertheless, yield significant results in reducing caseloads and workloads. Some argue that such efforts will not be effective without attention to caseload and workload (Children's Bureau, n.d., slide 15).

State and Local Examples of Caseload and Workload Strategies

State and local agencies throughout the country are using the strategies above to reduce caseloads and manage workloads. Following are selected examples.[1] While the examples below highlight certain aspects of a State's caseload/workload strategy, they may not provide the complete picture of that State's multifaceted initiative. Also, it is important to note that current economic conditions and budget crises are affecting many agencies' abilities to implement and sustain caseload and workload reduction. The following profiles represent point-in-time snapshots. As agencies respond to budget constraints and other environmental factors, activities and results may change.

- New Jersey: Infrastructure changes and case practice model

- Minnesota: Workload analytic tool

- Larimer County, CO: Workload reports and informed decision-making

- Indiana: Staff expansion, enrichment, and practice reform

- Delaware: Designated funding, overhiring pool, and staff retention

- Arizona: Staffing, staff development, and prevention

---

[1] The examples are presented for information purposes only; inclusion does not indicate an endorsement by the U.S. Department of Health and Human Services, Children's Bureau, or Child Welfare Information Gateway.

New Jersey: Infrastructure Changes and Case Practice Model

Caseload management has played a central role in New Jersey's recent reform efforts with an emphasis on infrastructure improvements. In response to a modified settlement agreement (MSA), *Charlie and Nadine H. v. Corzine*, the Department of Children and Families (DCF) was created as a standalone, cabinet-level department in 2006. DCF hired hundreds of new workers, implemented more comprehensive and timely training for frontline staff and supervisors, and provided critical supports.

To serve children and families more effectively, DCF introduced a case practice model. The model articulates the department's guiding values, integrates best practices, and identifies family engagement as a core strategy. DCF is implementing the case practice model incrementally through extensive instruction, coaching, and mentoring to selected immersion sites, as well as broader training statewide. Caseload management makes possible the time caseworkers need to apply the case practice model. In turn, using the case practice model to serve children and families more purposefully supports caseload management.

Enhanced data and management tools represent another element in New Jersey's caseload management efforts. Safe Measures, an analytic tool, pulls data from SACWIS and the NJ Spirit data system and provides managers, supervisors, and workers with access to a range of information including current caseload levels, completion of key case events, family contacts, and compliance with Federal requirements. Managers have used Safe Measures to track progress against

caseload standards set forth in the MSA, direct new staff and supports to identified areas of need, and distribute cases rationally across staff (DCF, 2007).

With a foundation of infrastructure, workforce, and service improvements in place, New Jersey entered the second phase of its massive reform effort in January 2009. Attention has shifted to sustainability, further institutionalizing the case practice model, developing quality review processes, and maintaining progress toward meeting specified outcome benchmarks and performance indicators.

Results: New Jersey has made substantial progress in achieving more manageable caseloads for caseworkers. In March 2006, more than 100 caseworkers in New Jersey had caseloads of more than 30 families; as of June 2009, no caseworkers had more than 30 families (DCF, 2009). According to a court-ordered independent monitor, in 2009 DCF achieved or exceeded the office average caseload standards set for intake workers (no more than 12 open cases and 8 new referrals per month), permanency workers (no more than 15 families and 10 children in out-of-home care at one time), and adoption workers (no more than 12 children). Individual caseload standards were met by 90 percent of all case-carrying staff. In addition, DCF showed significant improvements in child safety and placement outcomes (Center for the Study of Social Policy [CSSP], 2009).

The independent monitor credited New Jersey's caseload reduction with "beginning to make a difference in the quality of practice across the State, producing greater stability in the workforce, and creating an environment that provides staff the opportunity to follow

This material may be freely reproduced and distributed. However, when doing so, please credit Child Welfare Information Gateway. Available online at www.childwelfare.gov/pubs/case_work_management/

8

the principles articulated in the case practice model." (CSSP, 2008).

For more information, contact Kathleen Niedt, DCF, 609.292.9062, kathleen.niedt@dcf.state.nj.us

Minnesota: Workload Analytic Tool

The Minnesota Department of Human Services (MDHS) has developed an innovative and easy-to-use analytic tool to help counties manage their child welfare workloads. The tool, constructed using MS Excel, allows county directors, managers, and supervisors to enter caseload and workforce data and project staff needs. By using the tool over time, counties in this county-administered child welfare system can assess whether they are under- or over-staffed to handle cases properly and also whether the distribution of staff across case type is appropriate (Hornby Zeller Associates, Inc., 2009a).

Critical data inputs for the analytic tool were generated from a statewide child welfare workload study conducted in 2009 through a contract with Hornby Zeller Associates. The study was not intended to calculate a caseload standard, but rather to develop a better understanding of the time required for staff to conduct children and family workgroups (Minnesota's term for cases). The workload study collected data to measure two types of time:

- **Staff time available for casework.** Through a random moment survey reflecting 4,000 random moments, staff in 40 counties were asked to report what they were working on. Survey results found that workers spent approximately two-thirds of their time on case-specific work (Hornby Zeller Associates, 2009b).

- **Average time spent on cases.** Under a case time study, workers recorded the time spent on various tasks for a sample of 2,155 cases. This information was used to calculate how much time was needed to handle different types of cases in accordance with State and Federal requirements.

Integrating the findings from both sources into the analytic tool, Minnesota has developed an ongoing mechanism for tracking caseloads and generating indicators of resource needs. The State has introduced the tool to county administrators through a series of training webinars and continues to plan and implement additional training and one-on-one technical assistance.

Given the importance of a stable workforce to meaningful workload measures, Minnesota's workload study also addressed retention and the role of supervisors in supporting and retaining staff. Nearly 900 caseworkers, case aides, and supervisors completed staff surveys indicating reactions to statements about various topics associated with retention (e.g., agency policy, training, supervision). The survey findings are being used in planning the State's new Supervision Initiative.

Minnesota experienced high response rates in each of the workload study components. The random moment survey yielded a 99 percent response rate, and more than 84 percent of caseworkers completed the staff survey. Administrators attribute this success in large part to the upfront activities conducted to ensure buy-in at the county level (C. Borsheim, personal communication, Jan. 13, 2010). These activities included inviting county directors to be part of the workload study advisory group, assigning "champions" in specific sites to oversee data collection, and clearly communicating the objectives and intended uses of the study. For examples of MDHS communication soliciting participation among county staff, see Minnesota Child Welfare Workload Study Memos (Minnesota Department of Human Services, 2009).

Results: Minnesota recognized that while it was introducing a number of new practice reforms, training initiatives, and quality assurance improvements, these efforts would have little effect with an inadequate workforce. While it is too early to assess their effects, recent workload management efforts are important steps to stabilizing the workforce. The workload study has helped MDHS gain a better understanding of how to measure staffing levels needed to provide quality services, which in turn provides a foundation for resource management and financing decisions. The recently introduced analytic tool has been well received by county administrators who described it as "awesome" and found it useful in considering staff workloads.

For more information, contact Christeen Borsheim, MDHS, 651.431.3857, christeen.borsheim@state.mn.us

Larimer County, CO: Workload Reports and Informed Decision-Making

In Larimer County, CO, workload reports serve as a tool to make informed decisions on work distribution and staff allocation. These reports have helped administrators and supervisors recognize where staffing needs are greatest and respond accordingly. Workload efforts also have supported other reform initiatives related to differential response,

family team meetings, service delivery, and deinstitutionalization.

Using data from an internal time study coupled with other State and county workload studies, Larimer County developed time standards for assessments and ongoing services. These standards incorporated time for family meetings and travel and also reflect time adjustments for cases with multiple children and placement changes (Drendel & Suniga, 2008). The standards are integrated into the statewide information system, and weekly reports present workloads for every worker.

Larimer County administrators and supervisors use these workload reports to assess and redistribute ongoing work. In some instances, managers have moved staff from one unit with a lower workload to another with a higher workload. Based on workload reports, changes also have been made to the composition of paired teams implementing differential response (adding one intake worker and reducing one ongoing worker for each team). Presented with data from workload reports that highlighted the need for more upfront support, supervisors and staff readily accepted reallocation changes.

Results: Larimer County's workload reports have resulted in more equitable distribution of casework. They also have provided supervisors and program managers with tools for enhanced staffing and program decisions, supporting the implementation of differential response and deinstitutionalization. In addition, workload efforts have contributed to positive safety outcomes for children. For example, according to Jim Drendel, manager of the Larimer County Children, Youth & Family Division, maltreatment recurrence has dropped from over 10 percent in 2007 to below 4 percent in 2009 (J. Drendel, personal communication, Feb. 8, 2010).

For more information, contact Jim Drendel, Larimer County Department of Human Services, Children, Youth & Family Division, 970.498.6990, jdrendel@larimer.org

Indiana: Staff Expansion, Enrichment, and Practice Reform

With Indiana caseloads at times exceeding 50 children per worker, a statewide stakeholder group—the Indiana Commission on Abused and Neglected Children and Their Families—issued recommendations to the General Assembly in 2004 to reduce caseloads to CWLA standards (Folaran, 2004). The election of a new governor that year provided the catalyst for commitments to reform and support the child protection system. The State passed the best practice standards, which included, among other systemic improvements, caseload standards.

In the following years, Indiana completed a large hiring wave, adding 800 family case manager positions to nearly double its frontline staff. The State hired an additional 150 supervisors and reorganized the statewide child protection administration through regionalization. The Indiana Statewide Assessment reported that the additional staff lowered caseloads for many of the State's family case managers (Children's Bureau, 2008b).

In addition, the Indiana Department of Child Services (DCS), established as a separate entity in 2005, redesigned its infrastructure, policies, and practices to support practice reform. The State's practice reform centers on a family engagement-focused practice

model emphasizing five core skills—teaming, engaging, assessing, planning, and intervening (TEAPI). Administrators expect that this reform will "have long-term positive effects for children and families leading to shorter lengths of stay [in the child welfare system] and faster reunification or permanence, which will ultimately reduce caseloads" (DCS, 2009a).

Reinforcing the practice model and caseload reduction efforts, DCS launched multiple initiatives focused on training, staff enrichment, and retention:

* Enhanced pre-service training, which offers less classroom work and more on-the-job training and "transfer of learning"

* Field mentor program matching each trainee with an experienced family case manager who provides one-on-one assistance and structured feedback

* Supervisor initiative to improve supervisor-employee relationships with an emphasis on building communication and feedback skills

* Comprehensive exit interview tool that captures reasons for turnover and informs hiring and retention practices

Indiana also developed caseload management software to allow managers to assign assessments and ongoing cases according to best practice standards. In the coming years, the State plans to establish a caseload weighting system to more accurately reflect workloads and allow managers to distribute work and set expectations more effectively (DCS, 2009b).

Results: As of June 2009, 16 of 18 Indiana regions (89 percent) met the caseload standards of no more than 12 active cases related to initial assessments/investigations and 17 ongoing cases. Turnover of family case managers decreased to 16 percent (DCS, 2009a). The State also observed steady improvements in monthly caseworker visits and improved permanency outcomes on CFSR composite measures.

For more information, contact James Payne, Indiana DCS, 317.234.1391, james.payne@dcs.in.gov

Delaware: Designated Funding, Overhire Pool, and Staff Retention

Challenged by high staff turnover rates and concerns over well-publicized child fatalities, Delaware adopted an aggressive approach to managing caseloads that encompasses legislative support to meet caseload standards, hiring strategies, and initiatives to more effectively prepare and retain workers. Supported by legislation enacted in 1998 and 2004 and amended in 2007, Delaware set caseload standards (currently 11 cases for investigation workers and 18 for treatment workers) as well as supervisor standards (five family services workers per supervisor).

The legislation further tied allocation and funding of new positions to these caseload standards. Each year, based on projections of child abuse and neglect cases, the General Assembly is authorized to fund adequate staff so that caseloads do not exceed the established standards.

In a related innovative hiring strategy, the Division of Family Services (DFS) established an "overhire pool" to fill vacancies quickly and stabilize caseloads. For up to 15 positions, the agency assigns two people to one budget position slot. Overhires are available

immediately to step into a position when a worker resigns. They also carry cases while newly hired workers focus on training, fill in temporarily during a maternity or medical leave, and receive assignments to units experiencing high fluctuations in cases.

In addition, Delaware also implemented several other recruitment, retention, and training efforts:

- Establishing a new career ladder with additional job categories for family service workers that enabled promotional opportunities
- Increasing salaries for workers with more than 1 year of experience
- Introducing a rapid replacement process for new workers, which draws on continuous interviewing and a hiring waiting list
- Expanding pre-service training to 125 hours and implementing formal mentoring and shadowing programs for new workers before they receive cases
- Providing enhanced supervisor training, setting competency-based performance expectations, and engaging supervisors in turnover prevention

These efforts were intended to keep staff levels stable and thereby better control caseloads.

DFS administrators attribute the involvement of community partners to their success in caseload management and reduced turnover (S. Roberts, personal communication, Feb. 5, 2010). In particular, the multidisciplinary Child Protection Accountability Commission has been instrumental in advocating for needed change.

Results: Overhire and rapid replacement processes reduce the impact of turnover by allowing a trained person to step into a vacancy as soon as it is announced and by reducing the need to redistribute caseloads or interrupt service delivery (DFS, 1999). Following implementation of the above workforce initiatives, staff turnover dropped substantially from approximately 48 percent in 1998 to 8 percent in 2009 (DFS, 2010).

Delaware child welfare caseloads are monitored monthly against standards. In 2009, based on fully functional workers, statewide investigation caseloads averaged approximately 13 (slightly above standard), while statewide treatment caseloads fell below the caseload standard of 18 (DFS, 2010). Based on progress evident in its CFSR, Delaware's initiatives earned it recognition as a Children's Bureau Promising Approach in Child Welfare.

For more information, contact Shirley Roberts, Delaware DFS, 302.633.2601, Shirley. Roberts@state.de.us

Arizona: Staffing, Staff Development, and Prevention

Between 2000 and 2010, Arizona's Department of Economic Security (DES) implemented several initiatives related to workload management. Many of these initiatives were sparked by then-Governor Janet Napolitano's Action Plan for Reform of Arizona's Child Protection System and supported by legislation passed during a 2003 Arizona Legislature Special Session (Napolitano, 2003).

As called for under the new legislation (HB 2024), Arizona established State-specific caseload standards. To inform these

standards, a workgroup assessed the time needed to perform casework activities in Arizona in accordance with identified best practices (Costello, 2004). While the ideal best practice estimates were not fiscally viable, new standards were set in 2004, significantly below Arizona's prior caseload levels. The new standards called for a maximum caseload of 10 investigations, 19 in-home cases, and 16 children in out-of-home care.

To reduce caseloads and strengthen its workforce, Arizona implemented multiple strategies, which coincided with reforms outlined in the Division of Children, Youth and Family's (DCYF) *Strengthening Families—A Blueprint for Realigning Arizona's Child Welfare System* (DES, 2005). Multifaceted initiatives included:

- **Additional staff.** More than 375 new caseworker positions were authorized between 2003–2008, resulting in an approximate 50 percent increase.

- **Recruitment and hiring strategies.** While the State was actively recruiting new workers, it expanded employee benefits to include increased salaries and stipends for bilingual staff, workers with master's degrees in social work, workers in rural areas, and frontline investigators. (Due to budget cuts, these stipends have since been discontinued.) In addition, the State introduced a competency-based recruitment model and began offering a realistic job preview to promote better "fit" for new hires.

- **Training and staff development.** The State's Child Welfare Institute developed and trained new case managers on its CORE curriculum, which combined classroom instruction with use of prototype cases, simulations, and hands-on activities, followed by field training. In addition, a partnership with the Arizona State School of Social Work supports classes and supervised casework experiences for social work students and potential DCYF employees.

- **Supervisor initiatives.** Recognizing the link between supervision and retention, the State developed enhanced supervisor training and strengthened clinical supervision practices.

- **Prevention and early intervention.** Arizona introduced a major Family to Family initiative, focused on team decision-making, recruiting resource families, and building community partnerships. This strategy is intended to safely reduce the number of children in out-of-home care, thereby reducing caseloads. Arizona also expanded its Healthy Families program and offered an array of contracted in-home services to link at-risk children and families to needed services.

The sustainability of Arizona's workload management efforts has been challenged by the current economic environment. DCYF budget cuts have led to the suspension of some of the above programs, layoffs among 150 frontline workers in 2009, a hiring freeze, and severe reductions in prevention and family support services. At the same time, economic factors create additional stress on families and increase factors that place children at risk of maltreatment (DES, 2010). With the decrease in funded positions, the State is no longer staffed to meet casework standards.

Results: Arizona's initiatives have strengthened its capacity to attract, prepare, and support its frontline staff. While the impact on outcomes

is not clear, improvements have been reported in the number of children in foster care and their parents receiving required contact with case managers (Children's Bureau, 2008a). Additionally, the expansion in prevention and in-home services appears to have had a positive effect on reducing repeat maltreatment reports (DCYF staff, personal communication, Feb. 12, 2009).

Initially, as staff numbers increased, Arizona experienced progress in reducing caseloads. However, budget cuts and unfunded positions, along with State increases in maltreatment reports, currently contribute to higher caseload levels. During the period July–December 2008, CPS specialists were carrying caseloads that were on average 19 percent above the caseload standard (DES, 2009).

For more information, contact Jakki Hillis, DES, DCYF, 602.542.3598, JHillis@azdes.gov

Related Resources and Services of the Children's Bureau

Child Welfare Workload Compendium

This database on Child Welfare Information Gateway provides child welfare administrators and policymakers with information and tools for improving workload management, including studies, standards, legislation, and policies. It can be searched by State, category, date, and keyword.

This material may be freely reproduced and distributed. However, when doing so, please credit Child Welfare Information Gateway. Available online at www.childwelfare.gov/pubs/case_work_management/

14

National Child Welfare Workforce Institute

Works to build the capacity of the child welfare workforce by disseminating information on effective and promising workforce practices, facilitating leadership training, coordinating peer networks, and advancing knowledge. It partners with and coordinates evaluation activities of the Child Welfare Comprehensive Workforce Grants and supports the Child Welfare Workforce Connection, an online forum for discussion, collaboration, and exchange of ideas related to pressing workforce issues.

National Resource Center for Organizational Improvement

Helps States assess workforce development issues such as recruitment, selection, training, retention, and supervision, and helps them make connections with appropriate resources.

Child Welfare Information Gateway

Presents research, tools, and other resources that describe a range of topics for enhancing the child welfare workforce, including organizational culture, management, supervision, recruitment and hiring, and retention. Tools for building a stable and competent workforce also are available.

Child Welfare Comprehensive Workforce Projects (Children's Bureau Discretionary Grants)

Summarizes project activities, findings, and products from 2003–2008 child welfare staff recruitment and retention grantees, and is found in *Recruitment and Retention of a Qualified Workforce: The Foundation of*

Success. Information on current child welfare workforce projects is available at http://ncwwi. org/projects.htm

National Resource Center for Child Protective Services

Addresses workload issues and provides expert consultation, technical assistance, and training in all areas of child protective services, including intake, assessment, case planning, ongoing safety management, removal and reunification decision making, ongoing services, and case closure.

National Resource Center for Child Welfare Data and Technology

Offers States a wide range of technical assistance and products to enhance data analysis capacities, including support for monitoring and managing workload data.

National Resource Center for Permanency and Family Connections

Provides States with training, technical assistance, and information services related to family-centered principles and practices. Products include Information Packet: Workforce Issues in Child Welfare.

Other Resources

American Humane Association

Offers consultation and services in workload measurement and analysis. Prior workload studies are accessible on its website.

Child Welfare League of America

Publishes best practice and caseload standards and advocates for policies and practices that strengthen the workforce.

Cornerstones for Kids

Manages the Human Services Workforce Initiative, supported by the Annie E. Casey Foundation, with the aim of increasing awareness of the child welfare workforce crisis and building solutions to address it. It also operates the Workforce Planning Portal, a hands-on tool for human services agencies.

References

Alliance for Children and Families, American Public Human Services Association, and Child Welfare League of America. (2001). The child welfare workforce challenge: Results from a preliminary study. Retrieved December 2, 2009, from www.alliance1. org/Research/Workforce%20survey%20 results%20-%20final.PDF

American Public Human Services Association. (2005). *Report from the 2004 Child Welfare Workforce Survey: State agency findings.* Retrieved December 2, 2009, from www. aphsa.org/Home/Doc/Workforce%20 Report%202005.pdf

Arizona Department of Economic Security, Division of Children, Youth and Families. (2005). *Strengthening families: A blueprint for realigning Arizona's child welfare system.* Retrieved November 30, 2009, from https:// egov.azdes.gov/CMS400Min/InternetFiles/ Reports/pdf/strengthening_families.pdf

Arizona Department of Economic Security, Division of Children, Youth and Families. (2009). *Child protective service bi-annual financial and program accountability report.* Retrieved February 12, 2010, from www. azdes.gov/CMS400Min/InternetFiles/ Reports/pdf/financial_program_ accountability_report_cps_2009_1.pdf

Arizona Department of Economic Security, Division of Children, Youth and Families. (2010). *Child welfare reporting requirements: Semi-annual report for the period April 1, 2009 through September 30, 2009.* Retrieved February 12, 2010, from www.azdes.gov/CMS400Min/InternetFiles/ Reports/pdf/child_welfare_apr_09_sept_09. pdf

Bernotavicz, F. (2008). *Screening and selection of child welfare staff.* Retrieved February 17, 2010, from the Child Welfare Training Institute website: www.cwti.org/ RR/Screening%20and%20selection%20 Final%206-08%201.pdf

Center for the Study of Social Policy. (2008). *Progress of New Jersey Department of Children and Families. Period V monitoring report for Charlie and Nadine H. v. Corzine.* (July 1–December 31, 2008). Retrieved November 30, 2009, from www.childrensrights.org/wp-content/ uploads//2009/04/2009-04-27_nj_ monitoring_report_final_corrected.pdf

Center for the Study of Social Policy. (2009). *Progress of New Jersey Department of Children and Families. Period VI monitoring report for Charlie and Nadine H. v. Corzine.* (January 1–June 30, 2009). Retrieved January 7, 2010, from www.cssp.org/

uploadFiles/FINAL%20Period%20VI%20 Monitoring%20Report.pdf

Children's Bureau, U.S. Department of Health and Human Services. (n.d.). Strategies that address critical practice areas: Successes and challenges in implementation. PowerPoint presentation. Retrieved March 16, 2010, from www.acf.hhs.gov/programs/ cb/cwmonitoring/strategies/sld001.htm

Children's Bureau, U.S. Department of Health and Human Services. (2006). *Summary of the results of the 2001–2004 Child and Family Services Reviews.* Retrieved March 16, 2010, from www.acf.hhs.gov/programs/ cb/cwmonitoring/results/index.htm

Children's Bureau, U.S. Department of Health and Human Services. (2008a). *Arizona Child and Family Services Review: Final report.* Retrieved November 30, 2009, from http:// tinyurl.com/5b2syc

Children's Bureau, U.S. Department of Health and Human Services. (2008b). *Indiana Child and Family Services Review: Final report.* Retrieved March 16, 2010, from http:// tinyurl.com/ychhos8

Children's Defense Fund and Children's Rights, Inc. (2006). *Supporting and improving the child welfare workforce: A review of Program Improvement Plans (PIPs) and recommendations for strengthening the Child and Family Services Reviews (CFSRs).* Retrieved October 30, 2009, from www. childrensdefense.org/child-research-data-publications/data/supporting-and-improving-the-child-welfare-workforce.pdf

Costello, T. (2004). *Final report of the Investigation Caseload Standard Workgroup.* Retrieved October 30, 2009, from http://library.childwelfare.gov/cwig/ ws/library/docs/gateway/Record?rpp=10&u pp=0&m=1&w=+NATIVE%28%27recno%3 D49707%27%29&r=1

Day, P., & Peterson, C. (2008). *Caseload reduction efforts in selected States.* Unpublished manuscript, Casey Family Programs and ICF International.

Delaware Children's Department. (2010). *Caseworker turnover.* Unpublished.

Delaware Children's Department. (1999). *Enhancing workforce effectiveness through retention. Budget epilogue.* Unpublished.

Drendel, J., & Suniga, D. (2008, December). *Larimer County Workload versus Caseload Project.* Paper presented at the conference Time and Effort: Perspectives on Workload Roundtable. Santa Fe, NM.

Edwards, M. T., & Reynolds, J. (2008). Work, case, time: Setting standards for workload management. *Protecting Children,* 23(3), 74-88.

Ellet, A. J., Ellet, C. D., & Rugutt, J. K. (2003). *A study of personal and organizational factors contributing to employee retention and turnover in child welfare in Georgia: Final project report.* Unpublished. Athens: University of Georgia.

Farber, J., & Munson, S. (2007). *Improving the child welfare workforce: Lessons learned from class action litigation.* Retrieved October 30, 2009, from the National Center

for Youth Law website: www.youthlaw.org/
publications/improving_the_child_welfare_
workforce_lessons_learned_from_class_
action_litigation

Flower, C., McDonald, J., & Sumski, M. (2005).
*Review of turnover in Milwaukee County:
Private agency child welfare ongoing case
management staff.* Retrieved November
27, 2009, from the Wisconsin Department
of Children and Families website: www.
legis.state.wi.us/lc/committees/study/2008/
SFAM08/files/turnoverstudy.pdf

Folaron, G., (Ed.) (2004). *Putting children
first: Recommendations from the Indiana
Commission on Abused and Neglected
Children and Their Families.* Retrieved
November 27, 2009, from www.in.gov/
legislative/igareports/agency/reports/
ANCH01.pdf

Gonzalez, R. P., Faller, K. C., Ortega, R. M.,
& Tropman, J. (2009). Exit interviews with
departed child welfare workers: Preliminary
findings. *Journal of Public Child Welfare,
(3)*1, 40-63.

Hornby Zeller Associates, Inc. (2009a).
*Statewide Workload Analytic Tool:
User's reference guide.* Prepared for
Minnesota Department of Human Services.
Unpublished.

Hornby Zeller Associates, Inc. (2009b). *Child
Welfare Workload Study and Analysis. Final
report.* Prepared for Minnesota Department
of Human Services. Unpublished.

Indiana Department of Child Services.
(2009a). *Quarterly report to the Indiana
State Budget Committee and the Indiana*

*Legislative Council. For the Quarter Ended
6/30/09.* Retrieved November 27, 2009,
from www.in.gov/legislative/igareports/
agency/reports/DCS18.pdf

Indiana Department of Child Services. (2009b).
*State Five Year Comprehensive Child and
Family Service Plan for the State of Indiana
for the time period beginning October 1,
2009 and ending September 30, 2014.*
Submitted to the U.S. Department of
Health and Human Services, Administration
for Children and Families, Children's
Bureau.

Juby, C., & Scannapieco, M. (2007).
Characteristics of workload management
in public child welfare agencies.
Administration in Social Work, 31(3),
95-109.

Levy credits foster care avoidance for
generating $5 million in 2009 savings:
Excellent child protective services
management averts foster care reduces
caseload by 26 percent. (2009, September
25). *Hamptons.com For the Record.*
Retrieved September 26, 2009, from
www.hamptons.com/News/For-The-
Record/9014/Levy-Credits-Foster-Care-
Avoidance-For-Generating.html

Minnesota Department of Human Services.
(2009). Minnesota child welfare workload
study memos. Retrieved March 16, 2010,
from http://basis.caliber.com/cwig/ws/
library/docs/gateway/Blob/66865.pdf?w=+
NATIVE%28%27recno%3D66865%27%29&
upp=0&rpp=10&r=1&m=1

Napolitano, J. (2003). *Action plan for reform of
Arizona's child protection system.* Retrieved

February 12, 2010, from the Arizona Governor website: http://azgovernor.gov/cps/documents/action_plan3.pdf

National Council on Crime and Delinquency. (2006). *The relationship between staff turnover, child welfare system functioning and recent child abuse.* Retrieved October 30, 2009, from the Cornerstones for Kids website: www.cornerstones4kids.org/images/nccd_relationships_306.pdf

New Jersey Department of Children and Families. (2007). *Implementing the case practice model.* Retrieved February 6, 2010, from www.state.nj.us/dcf/about/case/DCFImplementingCPM9.28.07.pdf

New Jersey Department of Children and Families. (2009). *Annual agency performance report. Fiscal year 2009.* Retrieved January 6, 2010, from www.state.nj.us/dcf/about/DCFAnnualAgencyPerformanceReport_12.15.09.pdf

Payne, J. (2008, December). Getting from A to Z: Steps for improving child and family outcomes through caseload/workload reduction. Presentation at the Workload Round Table, Santa Fe, NM.

Social Work Education Consortium. (2002). Workforce retention study. November 25, 2009, from the New York State Office of Children and Family Services website: www.ocfs.state.ny.us/ohrd/swec/pubs/Executive% 20Summary%20-%20Quantitative%20Final.pdf

Strolin, J., McCarthy, M., & Caringi, J. (2007). Causes and effects of child welfare

workforce turnover: Current state of knowledge and future directions. Journal of Public Child Welfare, 1(2), 29-52.

Tooman, G., & Fluke, J. D. (2002). Beyond caseload: What workload studies can tell us about enduring issues in the workplace. Protecting Children, 17(3), 48-59.

U.S. General Accounting Office. (2003). Child welfare: HHS could play a greater role in helping child welfare agencies recruit and retain staff. Retrieved October 30, 2009, from www.gao.gov/new.items/d03357.pdf

Wagner, D., Johnson, K., & Healy, T. (2008). Agency workforce estimation: A step toward more effective workload management. Protecting Children, 23(3), 6-19. Retrieved March 16, 2010, from www.nccd-crc.org/crc/crc/pubs/americanHumane_agency_workforce_estimation.pdf

Zlotnik, J. L., DePanfilis, D., Daining, C., & Lane, M. M. (2005). Factors influencing retention of child welfare staff: A systematic review of research. Retrieved October 30, 2009, from the Institute for the Advancement of Social Work Research website: www.charityadvantage.com/iaswr/FinalReportCWWI.pdf

CPSIA information can be obtained
at www.ICGtesting.com
Printed in the USA
LVHW101711210220
647795LV00006B/258